up NEPA

GIWA OLAKUNLE LOUKMAN

UP N.....................EPA

Copyright © 2018

by GIWA OLAKUNLE LOUKMAN

ISBN 978-978-953-451-7

All rights reserved. Except as permitted under the Nigerian Copyright laws, no part of this publication may be reproduced, distributed, or transmitted in any form or by any means, or stored in a database or retrieval system, without the prior written permission of the author.

Published by:
Creative World Productions Ltd
Tel: +234 803 580 3344, 0802 303 8830
Email: kunle_giwa@yahoo.com
cwpnigeria2018@gmail.com

Design, Inner Layout and Printing:
EFX CREATIONS
4b Bola Street, Anthony Lagos.
Tel: +234 806 053 4898
Email: sam@efxcreations.com
Website: www.efxcreations.com

ACKNOWLEDGMENT

First and foremost, I give thanks, glory and adoration to God Almighty for being there for me throughout my literary muse. I acknowledge my wife and children for their understanding whenever Daddy keeps away from home and keeps late nights in the course of this project.

My special appreciation goes to two like minds. Messrs Ekundayo Oriyomi Omole and Yemi Olumegbon who both mediated in the squabble between my publisher and I that almost dwarfed this project and who are also brains behind the original concept of the cover page design.

I acknowledge my respected lecturer of all times Prof. Ayo Akinwale (Weyler) for his invaluable tutelage back then in the university days. I appreciate the editing he made to this play and the incisive preface he wrote on it.

The suggestions made by Messrs Azeem Popoola and Bashir Sholadoye are highly valued not forgetting the meaningful contribution made by Mr. Goodman Shodeinde. All those personalities worthy of mention but who through stroke of my forgetfulness have their names omitted, I say "a thousand apologies".

Lastly, I acknowledge Almighty God, the Omnipotent, the Omniscience for the successful completion of this book.

DEDICATION

Dedicated to the memories of my late father M.O.A. Giwa

PREFACE

The fulfilment of a teacher is to see his pupils grow in the profession doing better than him. This is the case with Mr. Giwa Olakunle Loukman and I. When he was in the University, he paid specific attention to Theatre Practice and this script seems to be the product. Congratulations!

The play started with the quest of Mr. Oluyanju the lead character, wanting to travel abroad and leave his family behind. He fell asleep and entered a new World where everything seems to be working well. There was full light everywhere. He encountered a monster whom I interpreted is NEPA, Fought him and won. His later encounter with the same monster ended in him killing the monster and beheading him. The playwright's wish is that we will one day be out of our problems with NEPA and its lack of light.

Written in a simple and plain language, the play stimulates in us the true African Theatre where Drama is mixed with songs and dance. This is the African Total Theatre Model.

I therefore want to recommend this play not only to Theatre Scholars and students but to all Nigerians who feel that we are already enslaved by NEPA. One day will come when NEPA Issue will become History. I also recommend this play for Secondary School Students who are studying English Literature.

Thank you Mr. Giwa O Loukman. I am proud of you and your writing in this play. Please keep it up.

Professor Ayo Akinwale
Dean Faculty of Arts,
UNIVERSITY OF ILORIN 2016

CHARACTER PERSONAE

Oluyanju - Lead character

Adunni - Oluyanju's wife

Child 1 - Oluyanju's child

Child 2 - Oluyanju's 2nd child

Doctor - Oluyanju's family doctor

Neighbours 1 2 3 - Oluyanju's neighbours

Raku

Koro

king

Weirds

Mild ones

Chiefs

Masses

Bosses

(National Electric Power Authority. The Former body responsible for the supply of electricity in Nigeria)

ACT I SCENE I

A man comes back from office one day, calls his wife to share in his happiness that at long last, his visa request to U.S.A has been granted. The wife joins in the celebration. The children join in too. After praise songs, worship and thanks giving, they prepare his meal. The children ask him questions until he orders them to bed since tomorrow is another school day. As he is about to commence eating, light goes off.

A lavished sitting room with dinning area and a bar, a step unit leading to the bedroom upstage center, a set of cushion chairs with a center table, a telephone on a stool beside a flower vase depicting the room of an average country man. However, the vivid description of the sitting room can be done away with for ease of convenience in the change of scene situation. A large backdrop describing the room may suffice.

Oluyanju comes home from work and relays his experience in the office to his wife and children.

Oluyanju: Honey, I'm home!

Adunni: Welcome back home, sweetie.

Oluyanju: Do you not notice that I'm elated somehow?

Adunni: Ah, I wonder, but I didn't want to be forward.

Oluyanju: It calls for celebration

Adunni: What are you talking about?

Oluyanju:	I say it calls for celebration.
Adunni:	What calls for celebration?
Oluyanju:	My new found joy.
Adunni:	Then let's share it but remember there are only two of us here to celebrate
Oluyanju:	We will invite other people.
Adunni:	Is it that serious?
Oluyanju:	Yes, it is.
Adunni:	In that case, we have the children around to join us in the celebration.
Oluyanju:	Still not enough.
Adunni:	Then, we'll invite neighbors. But for God's sake, let me off the hook of suspense.
Oluyanju:	You will hear it, never mind.
Adunni:	Now, please.
Oluyanju:	Okay, okay, your majesty, this is it.
Adunni:	Where is it?
Oluyanju:	My VISA request to America (U S A) has been granted finally!
Adunni:	Heyyyyyy!!!
Olayunju:	Hey quiet. Now you are shouting.
Adunni:	Allow me.
Olayunju:	No!

Adunni:	Why no?
Oluyanju:	You'll distract neighbours.
Adunni:	Let me distract them.
Oluyanju:	No, you won't.
Adunni:	Yes, I will.
Oluyanju:	I said no.
Adunni:	I'm saying yes.
Oluyanju:	Why are you disregarding me?
Adunni:	You said we will need the neighbours to share in our joy.
Oluyanju:	Yes I did.
Adunni:	And I am summoning them.
Oluyanju:	Not in that uncouth fashion.
Adunni:	The children too will soon be here.
Oluyanju:	It is polite if you walk up to them to seek their audience.
Adunni:	(Talking seriously now). You mean the white guys finally stamped a visa on your passport?
Oluyanju:	Yes.
Adunni:	Then, I must glance at it at once.
Oluyanju:	(Searches his folder for it and when he sees it, he brings it out saying) here it is.

Adunni:	(Collecting it to inspect). You mean this is a genuine American Visa?
Oluyanju:	Yes of course. Would I be deceived into taking a counterfeit?
Adunni:	(Shouting and jumping up that the children appear to inquire). Heyyyyyy!!!

(The children appear from the room)

Children:	Mummy, what is the matter?
Oluyanju:	Adunni, you are shouting again and I don't like it.
Children:	Welcome Daddy!
Oluyanju:	Welcome my children.
Children:	What happened to mummy?
Oluyanju:	Your children are talking to you.
Adunni:	(Still dancing around). You say what?
Child I:	Why are you shouting? We thought you warned us not to shout in this house again.
Adunni:	Yes o my children.
Child II:	Then why are you doing that which you barred us from doing and attracting our neighbours?
Adunni:	Forgive me children.
Child II:	You are forgiven.
Adunni:	It is your father.
Child II:	What did our father do?

Adunni:	He brought home good news that one cannot help, but shout on.
Child I:	(Turning to Daddy) What good news did you bring Daddy?
Oluyanju:	That is the good news in her hand.
Adunni:	Your daddy has an American Visa which means he will be going to America very soon.
Child I:	Okay.
Adunni:	You see now why I have to shout.
Children:	But.....
Adunni:	There is no but there, my dear.
Oluyanju:	Honestly, I'm surprised.
Adunni:	You don't have to be, sweetie.
Oluyanju:	You will not admit your guilt yet you want the children to always own up theirs forgetting that you are a model to them.
Adunni:	Alright, alright, and alright.
Oluyanju:	Alright what?
Adunni:	I'm sorry, I admit I over reacted.
Oluyanju & Children:	Apology accepted!
Adunni:	Scores settled?
Oluyanju:	Yes.
Adunni:	I can now pour some wine.

Oluyanju:	Hen-hen, you can invite anybody under the sun now.
Child II:	Mummy, daddy has been travelling before. Why is this one being celebrated?
Adunni:	USA is referred to as the God's own country.
Child II:	Who owns our own country?
Adunni:	It is the same God.
Children:	So?
Adunni:	So, it is a land of opportunities
Child I:	Daddy, is it true?
Oluyanju:	Yes, your mummy is right.
Child II:	What makes USA different from other countries?
Adunni:	Will the children and father excuse me to go and set the table?
Children:	You may go.
Oluyanju:	Your children have answered you.
Adunni:	(Taking a bow as she goes). Thank you your majesties.
Oluyanju:	USA is a land of opportunities
Child I:	Mummy said the same thing.
Child II:	Does it mean opportunities do not abound in other countries that you have visited?

Child I:	Or is there no opportunity in our own 'God's own country' Nigeria?
Oluyanju:	In the United States of America, there exists the largest pool of races.
Children:	What does race mean?
Child I:	Do they run fast there?
Child II:	Are you going to race there?
Oluyanju:	You see, by races I mean different nationals e.g. Indians, Black Africans, Brown Asians, White Europeans, the Arabs and the Jews.
Child I:	Do they live there?
Oluyanju:	Yes, they do.
Child II:	Are you going to live there too?
Oluyanju:	Yes, I am.
Child I:	Can't you people live in your own countries?
Oluyanju:	We can. But because of the presence of all species of humans created by God in the country, God's presence is felt there more and because of the reverence they give to God despite their successes and excesses.
Children:	How does one know that the presence of God is somewhere?
Oluyanju:	Their economy, i.e. their buying and selling will be very good, that they will have money to do things like motors, Aeroplanes, Trains, ships,

	Submarines. They will travel to the moon to observe holidays.
Child I:	They will do generator too.
Child II:	Their "Up NEPA" will be stable.
Adunni:	Food is ready. Table is set.
Oluyanju:	Thank you honey.
Adunni:	The children are keeping you busy
Oluyanju:	In fact, they've almost set an exam for me.
Adunni:	You better hurry up, eat your food and run to bed.

) Food is laid on the table with fruits and juices. They eat, drink and toast to their father's success.)

Child I:	Daddy!
Oluyanju:	Yes, baby.
Child I:	You said you will go and stay in USA.
Oluyanju:	Yes.
Child I:	You will not come back home to us again?
Adunni:	He will come.
Child II:	When?
Child I:	He will stay there like other nationals.
Child II:	Who will look after us when you are gone?
Oluyanju:	Your mummy will remain with you.
Children:	Who will look after mummy?

Child I:	Who will give her money?
Oluyanju:	I will remit money home regularly.
Child II:	Can't all of us go and live in the United States of America?
Oluyanju:	We can.
Child I:	Hen-hen let everybody go.
Oluyanju:	It is not as easy as that. That is why we are celebrating the visa they gave me.
Child II:	What is visa?
Oluyanju:	(Beckons on the wife to bring the passport). It is the authority they give you to enter their country.
Adunni:	(presents it) here my dear
Oluyanju:	This is the visa (opens to the page where the visa is embossed)
Children:	Heeeeey! It is fine.
Oluyanju:	Yes, it is fine.
Adunni:	He needs to collect it for all of us if we want to go to USA.
Children:	Let him collect it now.
Oluyanju:	It is not easy like that
Adunni:	You don't understand.
Oluyanju:	Okay, thank you. It's time for bed. We will continue next time. `You know there's school

tomorrow.

(The children obey and leave for their room)

Adunni: Eat your food.

Oluyanju: Ah, the children are brainteasers.

Adunni: You need red wine now or after meal?

Oluyanju: Let me try perhaps I can gain my appetite back. *(He opens the bowl of Soup, takes a meat, savours it, and begins to help himself, he takes the rice from another bowl to a flat dish saucer. As he's about to pour the stew, NEPA 'strikes', light goes off).* Goodness me! Honey, kindly get me an alternative light please.

Adunni: It shall be done.

Oluyanju: Thanks.

Adunni goes to fetch a candle light. In a little while, she comes back on set with the light.

Adunni: Let me move it close to you so that you will see clearly what you are eating but first, let me place it on a candle stand.

Oluyanju: You see this country

Adunni: Are you telling me? Pilots term our country 'the darkest spot in the world'. They say once they arrive the air space & territory of this country they know they are in. No other country gives them that darkness feel, one time they recognize they are in Nigeria.

Oluyanju: And they say one should not say bad things about

	his country.
Adunni:	Then let the authority do the right things we will talk about
Oluyanju:	You think anybody that leaves this country in this kind of situation will ever come back home?
Adunni:	When will this ever stop? Power outages in this time and age of our existence?.
Oluyanju:	Is it the dearth of qualified engineers that is the problem, or scientist or technologists?
Adunni:	With the kind of money we make on petroleum, and other rich endowments in this country.
Oluyanju:	*(Shouting angrily now)*. Don't the people in the helms of affair travel out to these developed countries? Don't they see that light dares not go there? Can't they emulate that? Oh God! *(Coughing)*
Adunni:	Easy sweetie, take it easy.
Oluyanju:	*(Coughing hard but still trying to talk)*. This country can turn an intelligent, powerful and a resourceful person to a moron. Tell me, a patient being operated upon in the theatre wouldn't he die with these outages? One can't preserve perishable goods in the refrigerator. Please tell me, Artisans whose professions are energy based, wouldn't they be redundant without light? Employment generation is lost through "Nepa's" inefficiency, a crying shame.
Adunni:	That is alright sweetie. You are loosing strength.

(She leads him out of the dining area to the couch. He is

choking now with the eyes red hot emitting hot tears. He coughs violently. His breath seized. The frightened wife rushes quickly to get him water, forces it down his throat, he struggles to drink yet his breath is no longer full as he grunts instead of breathing. He sweats profusely).

Adunni: Hey! My God. Hey Olu! Olu!! Olu!!! Hey Yanju! Please don't do this to me. Remember we both planned to raise this family together. I will suffer if you dump the mantle of responsibility on me,

(She takes her phone, dials the family doctor) Hello!

Doctor's V.O: Yes, who is on the line?

Adunni: Mrs Oluyanju.

Doctor's V.O: Oh! Sorry madam. I should have known.

Adunni: Please doctor, my husband is dying!

Doctor's V.O: No he will not die, tell me madam, calm down and tell me what the problem is so that I can prescribe a first aid treatment prior to my arrival in your house.

Adunni: Light went out in the house when he was eating and he began to curse and rain abuses on NEPA till he begins to choke and cough.

Doctor's V.O: A morsel of what he was eating must have entered his wind pipe. That's why it's not good to talk while eating or eat while sleeping. Allow him fresh air, press his chest and call his name. I'm in the neighbourhood.

Adunni: Thank you. Please come over quick. *(She goes to see the husband who is now lifeless. She dilates, mouth agape; she lifts his harm and drops it with no life in it. She rushes out of the*

	room to call on neighbours.) please help me.
Neighbour I:	Take it easy madam.
Neighbour II	*Goes to the lifeless body on the sofa).* Mr. Oluyanju. *(He calls his name into his ears; he blows air into his nostrils)* Mr. Oluyanju! Mr. Oluyanju!! *(He presses his chest)*
Adunni:	Yes, that is what the doctor said I should do but when I turned to him and he was lifeless, I lifted his arm, it was stone cold, I had to rush to invite you because it's beyond my capacity. *(Enters the doctor)*
Doctor:	How far?
Adunni:	Thanks for coming doctor. See my plight.
Doctor:	Did you do what I asked you to do to him?
Adunni:	I couldn't
Doctor:	Why not?
Adunni:	By the time I hung the phone and turned to him, he has been like this, so I rushed to call neighbours.
Doctor:	(Goes to feel his pulse, he feels his arm and feet and then his armpits. Then he turns to people to ask.) What did you do when you saw him like this?
Neighbour II:	I went to blow air into his nostrils and press his chest.
Doctor:	*(Heaves a sigh and clears his forehead,)* Well.
Adunni:	Well what?!

Sharp fade out.

ACT I SCENE II

The stage is set as a forest as indicated by the backdrop. While on stage proper, human props will station like trees. Played recorded sounds of birds in the grove, sounds of serene forest life will jolt Oluyanju to move frightfully among the artificial trees unsuspecting to him until they turn slowly to reveal their identities. He puts up a volte-face. The artificial trees terrify him, he refuses to be terrified. They engage him in a battle.

Weird I: You stand there looking like a confused human being

Weird II: What are you doing here?

Weird III: Don't you know this is a territory of the spirit beings?

Oluyanju: I don't know

Weird IV: Then how did you get here?

Oluyanju: That, I don't know too.

Weird I: You are a liar.

Oluyanju: No, I'm not.

Weird II: So, we are lying then.

Oluyanju:	I have not said that.
Weird I:	But you have alluded to it.
Oluyanju:	May be or maybe not.
Weird III:	What?!
Weird IV:	You dared to answer us like that?
Oluyanju:	Well, I don't know how else to answer you.
Weird I:	Tie him up.

(Other weird beings attempt to rush at him but he escapes from their grip. He makes to engage them in a wrestling bout).

Weird I:	So it is fight you want?
Weird III:	So you can fight.
Weird I:	Raku!
Weird II:	Master!
Weird I:	Discipline him.
Weird II:	No problem about that, master.
Oluyanju:	There is a problem o.
Weird II:	Let us find out.

(They begin to wrestle. In no time at all, Oluyanju has ravaged Raku mercilessly to the chagrin of other weird creatures.)

Weird I:	Well-done human, but you must defeat all of us before we can acknowledge you as a fighter.

	Koro!
Weird III:	Yes, master!
Weird I:	Deal with him.
Weird III:	It shall be done in due course.
Oluyanju:	In due course, you say?
Weird III:	We don't expect your comments.

(The wrestling bout takes effect and the two contestants sweat it out at the end of which Oluyanju again injured weird III.)

Weird I:	You have exhibited the traits of a valiant. We will not allow you to ravage us all in shame. You will now battle two of us together.
Oluyanju:	You are welcome.

(The battle begins again in earnest. They both struggle to upturn Oluyanju but he is too swift for them. He takes them by the neck and smashes their heads against the other heavily leaving them to crash on the floor with a bang. The earlier injured ones and the small ones amongst them (The pixies) beg Oluyanju not to kill them, that they are ready to do his biddings. Meanwhile one of them has already run off to God knows where)

Mild one:	Please we will respect you. Order us around; you will see us loyal to you.
Oluyanju:	You don't have any problem at all if you are not violent. Where did that one run to? (Pointing at the escaping (Pixie) weird one)
Weird:	May be, to summon our king.

Oluyanju: What?! Your king? to come and do what?

Weird: In our tradition, if a stranger comes around and conquers us in the manner in which you have just done, the king must be summoned to give the final battle.

Oluyanju: Battle?

Weird: Yes battle. That is why we don't just install anybody as king. He must be brave like you.

Oluyanju: In that case, no problem. Let us wait and expect him

(The said king appears from no distant a place dressed in his war regalia. He looks like Sango but bigger by far in frame and stature.)

Weird: That is our king coming.

Oluyanju: He is welcome. *(A little intimidated by the king's size)*

King: Where is the strange one?

Weird: Here my lord. *(Pointing at Oluyanju)*

King: *(To Oluyanju).* You are the brave one that comes to ravage my people right under my nose

Oluyanju: I just found myself here, I didn't know how I got here, and your people attempted to suppress me instead of being accommodating.

King: That's why you must bully them like this in their domain?

Oluyanju: I need to defend myself.

King:	For how long do you hope to do that?
Oluyanju:	For as long as I can possibly defend and protect myself.
King:	Okay, let's see how you defend yourself against me. Arrrrrh!!!!!!!!!!! (He roars like Sango, but instead of him emitting fire from the mouth like Sango, it is water that comes out from his mouth. This angers Oluyanju and gives him more confidence to withstand the king should he advance towards him.)
Oluyanju:	I'm not afraid of you.
King:	You are not afraid of me?!
Oluyanju:	No, I'm not.
King:	Then say your last prayers. From this moment, you are dead, man! (He advances towards Oluyanju mightily and Oluyanju dodges making the king fall face down)
Oluyanju:	Haven't I gotten you now? (He sits on the neck of the king and deals a death blow on his head and face till he becomes unconscious. The other weird couldn't go near him for fear that he may kill them with their king)
Weird:	Great king. Long may you reign in our midst as a King.
Oluyanju:	Strip him!
Weird:	As you're pleased your honour! We will do your wish.

Fade out

ACT II SCENE I
TRANSITION SCENE

Still in the grove, the man sleeps and wakes up. He sees that everything has changed from the forest situation he meets himself. He finds himself in a beautiful palace and he occupies it as the king. Fully bedecked in a king's attire attending to chiefs and subjects on matters of state.

(New King) Oluyanju: *(Sees people appearing from rocks and mountains)* Fellow countrymen, am I the only one seeing what I'm seeing?

Chiefs: What are you seeing our wonderful king?

Oluyanju: I don't know whether it is proper for me to voice it out.

Chiefs: Voice it out, you have all the rights to say and do anything on this issue.

Oluyanju: Heenh, I see, I mean, I see or maybe I should go back to sleep perhaps it's in my dream. When I live in real life, I will know which is which.

Chiefs: Honourable king, you are not living in any dream, you are alive. We can feel you.

Oluyanju: In that case, a word will not be too big that we use knives to slice it. It is the mouth we will employ to say it; I see people appearing from rocks and mountains.

Chiefs:	Urh! That?
Oluyanju:	Yes, that.
Chiefs:	That is the make of this specie of beings
Oluyanju:	Is that so?
Chiefs:	Yes that is so. Sometimes people walk on their heads, on their hands and sometimes on their sides.
Oluyanju:	*(Frightened but pretends)* Oh! I see. I should have known that.
Chiefs:	No problem. In the course of events, you'll see so many other things. Your palace guards and attendants will take you round the city to familiarize you with what you need to know. (To guards). Organize a befitting outing for our new king. Let him be acquainted with his subjects.
Guards:	With all manner of respect.
Chief 4:	Do it quickly. Don't let it be long.
Guards:	If you want it now, we will, if the king is ready.
Chief:	Great king, prepare to undertake a familiarization tour of our city
Oluyanju:	Now?
Chief 2:	Now!
Oluyanju:	In that case shall we go?
Chief 1:	It won't take long

(King descends from his throne; he is being joined by the chiefs' in full royal regalia. The palace guards lead the convoy out of the palace.)

Palace guards: (Shouting on top of their voices.) Ken ku keku eeeeeeeeeeeeeeeeeeeeeeee!

Chief 3: That is for you, Great king.

Oluyanju: Meaning what?

Chiefs: Meaning that the greatest person in our land is coming; make way for him.

Palace Guards: Ken ku keku wehhhhhhhh

Chiefs: That is for us. It means that the most respected chiefs in the land are on the way.

Oluyanju: That is beautiful

Chiefs: Great king.

(Exit all. Light fades)

(Enter king Oluyanju and entourage on their return from the tour.)

Oluyanju: Honestly, I did not know that you people have a beautiful city such as this.

Chiefs: Great king.

Oluyanju: As a matter of fact, I did not even know what was propelling our tour. In a jiffy, we have touched many places; we have seen many people, houses and beautiful sceneries.

Chiefs:	Great king.
Oluyanju:	You are a set of good people. The set that one will look forward to working with. See light everywhere; see how my palace is beautifully lit.
Chiefs:	Great King.
Oluyanju:	You are a set of great people too.
Chiefs:	Great King.
Oluyanju:	Honestly, your lights beat my imagination. What's the secret?
Chief 3:	It is not only light. Anything we want to do, we want to do right. That's the target everybody sets for himself.
Oluyanju:	That's very good. It's a virtue worth emulating. Anything you do, you strive to do it right
Chief 2:	You dare not make a mistake for the price you pay is disastrous.
Oluyanju:	Hahn hehn?
Chiefs:	Yes.
Oluyanju:	Thank you very much. You must be tired now.
Chief 4:	Tired, why? When you are not tired you want to kill us?
Olayanju:	No.

Light out

ACT II SCENE II

Same situation, the masses appear in the palace with their agitation because light suddenly goes off in the whole city. A feat that has never been experienced before in their existence which throws everybody off guard and into confusion. Oluyanju looks at his chiefs for succour. He wonders why they have to protest in spite of all the effectiveness of their system.

Chief 1: Great king, I was going to tell you the other time that this light you love so much is not functioning optimally.

Oluyanju: You mean it?

Chief 11: Yes, our king

Oluyanju: How else does it work?

Chief 111: Light used to be everywhere such that people think it will blind them.

Chief 1: Because of its inefficiency, that's why these people have come.

Masses: Yes our king, the energy people are playing with our lives. Most of our businesses that depend on it are beginning to dwindle.

Oluyanju: Never mind, we shall invite them to hear their

	own side of the story.
Mass 3:	It is because you are new in our midst.
Oluyanju:	Otherwise, what could have happened?
Mass 5:	We would have sacrificed the workers to our gods.
Oluyanju:	*(Taken aback)*. What?
Mass 6:	Yes.
Chief:	Great king; you see, on the issue of this light, a lot of neighboring villages patronize us because of it
Oluyanju:	It is your- I mean it is our tourist attraction
Chiefs:	Yes.
Mass 5:	Besides most of our daily endeavours are dependent on it
Chief 2:	It is our livewire
Oluyanju:	In that case, let us entertain no further delay Let the guards' go to summon the Electricity workers to know why they must embark upon this unpatriotic act
Chief 1:	Guards!
Guards:	Yes chief!
Chief:	Great king wants you to go now to summon the workers in the light company.
Guard:	All off them or only their bosses
Oluyanju:	Get their bosses

Guards:	We go now, Great king
Oluyanju:	Quickly before this saliva I spit on the floor dries up. *(Spits on the floor)*
Guard:	We will be back now.

(Exit guards)

Oluyanju:	My loyal chiefs, your, I mean our people can be angry.
Chief:	It is because our lives depend on it.
Oluyanju:	Yes, you are right. But in situation where with impunity, they just seize the electricity, and throw the whole city into total darkness and gloom.
Chiefs:	Eeeeeeeee! Eeeeeeee!! Eeeeeeeee!!! Great king don't even dream it. In fact, the mere mention of it by you makes me nauseate
Oluyanju:	You cannot have such a silly situation in your city?
Chiefs:	Never!
Mass 5:	How is that possible on earth?
Chief I:	Has anyone heard of a place on earth where that is practicable?
Chief II:	I doubt it so much
Chief III:	Our Great king is just teasing us.
Chief IV:	Since I was born, I have not experienced it before.
Chief V:	That will be tantamount to genocide.

(Enter the guards with electricity bosses)

Mass 1: You are welcome, but thank the new king for your luck.

Oluyanju: My dear workers, a report has reached me concerning your poor services

Boss 1: We are really helpless about the situation, Great king.

Masses: *(Becoming unruly.)* I wonder why the Great king should allow them to defend themselves.

Mass I: They should be dealt with customary to our tradition.

Mass II: Imagine the booming economy that puts smiles on everybody's face.

Mass III: Just because of some few inefficient people. Oh! No!

Mass IV: Great king, these people don't deserve a second chance

Mass I: Let us finish them here and now.

Mass II: They can be replaced.

Masses: A lot of people want to exhibit their talents where they are fumbling.

Mass IV: Even, if we can not get replacement here, we have enough money to hire foreign hands to do the job.

Masses: Our economy must not suffer on their account.

Mass I:	If you don't allow us to deal with them in accordance with our laid down custom, it may eventually affect your own job as a Great king.
Oluyanju:	Why me?
Mass V:	Because you are the head and you are equally perverting justice.
Oluyanju:	Me, perverting justice?
Masses:	Yes, you are perverting justice
Oluyanju:	To you, perverting justice is hearing your own version of the story and denying the other party a fair hearing?!
Masses:	The rule says anybody that runs foul of the expectations of the mass of the people shall be liable to prosecution by the people.
Oluyanju:	I say that must stop!
Masses:	You cannot come and stop our custom with a fiat like that.
Oluyanju:	And I dare say that your custom must be reversed.

A rowdy commotion ensues. The people almost turn the palace to a garage, hitting and breaking, talking like barbarians, wild, eager to explode on the electricity workers and the new king until the chiefs call them to order.

Chiefs:	Eeeeeeeeeeeeeeeiiiiiiiiiiii!!!
Masses:	Arh! *(As in fem, fem)*
Chief I:	Have you forgotten in a hurry that the king is not a push over king?

33

Chief II:	And that you stand in his presence to roar like this?
Chief III:	If he unleashes terror on all of you, can you withstand him?
Chief IV:	Remember our Native king Okosofoko was disgracefully defeated by him.
Chief V:	Have you forgotten or shall I continue to reel out to you the qualities we see in him before we crowned him our new king?

(On this line, he prostrated to the king and other chiefs and later the bosses and the masses)

Oluyanju:	Thank you very much my loyal chiefs.
Chiefs:	It is our pleasure.
Oluyanju:	Let it be known to them that any new king will always come with his own ideas. No two ideas are bound to be the same.
Chiefs:	We will do that Great king.
Oluyanju:	Let them know that an elder or a leader that listens to a party in a conflict and takes decision is a cruel leader. Therefore, my style shall be to give fair hearing to all warring parties in a conflict. It does not mean that they are not guilty or that their guilt will be covered. No! But just to ensure that an innocent soul does not carry the guilt of the wicked.
Chiefs:	Good talk, Great king.
Chief I:	May you live long to give us more of these wise talks.

Oluyanju:	Let the representatives of the electricity workers state their case.
Spokesman:	Great king, we thank you for this opportunity given to us.
Masses:	Go straight to the point
Chiefs:	Don't perambulate
Boss I:	Thank you all the same our king and the wonderful people of our land – Kenkukeku.
Masses:	Thank you. That's alright.
Boss II:	Our hands are tied in the issue of light.
Oluyanju:	Who tied your hands?
Boss III:	We don't mean it that way Great king.
Chief:	Then say what you mean and mean what you say.
Boss I:	The petroleum workers came to us that their petroleum products need to move fast in the market to enable them make more money.
Masses:	How does that affect you?
Boss II:	They want the light disrupted so that people will go for generators and use fuel and other petroleum products.
Masses:	What?!
Chiefs:	That's a lie.
Oluyanju:	Allow them.

Boss I:	The high and mighty in our midst here and in the city believe they should have a stake in the electricity sector
Chiefs:	No way!
Mass 6:	There is a way
Boss III:	The generator importers and distributors too are on our neck to do brisk business
Oluyanju:	Masses, did you hear them now? Otherwise, you would have sacrificed them wrongly.
Mass 2:	It is a revolution.
Oluyanju:	The blood of innocent citizens?
Mass 1:	We will get to the bottom of the matter. Let's go.

(Exit the masses)

Oluyanju:	Is the matter not clear now?
Chief 4:	In fact, you exposed what should be exposed.
Oluyanju:	How does one get to the people with whatever outcome we are able to fashion out?
Boss 2:	Our Great king.
Oluyanju:	Yes, my good people.
Boss 2:	We need your special protection to overcome in all these.
Oluyanju:	You should entertain no more fears.
Chief:	Great king

Oluyanju:	Yes.
Chief:	They are right, you must act fast in protecting them else.....
Oluyanju:	Why?
Boss1:	They believe there are some of us light workers who compromised the operation of the smooth working of the light because according to their allusions we see it as an opportunity to 'milk' the place dry without being caught.
Oluyanju:	But you have cleared yourselves.
Boss:	They are not satisfied.
Oluyanju:	In that case, I will send my chiefs to go and persuade them.
Boss:	We will appreciate that greatly.
Oluyanju:	My loyal chiefs, ensure that you placate the people so that they allow peace to reign.
Chiefs:	Great king! It shall be done.
Oluyanju:	Good night, everybody.
Chiefs & Bosses:	Good night our Great king. *(They prostrated)*

(Exeunt all)

ACT III SCENE I

Oluyanju sits on his throne to rummage on the happenings in the land. In a short while, he falls asleep. Before long, he has started dreaming. In this dream, he combats the king of the weird and defeats him.

Oluyanju: You again, how did you escape?

Monster: It's me again. I can't imagine ordinary you defeating me and taking my crown and kingdom.

Oluyanju: In that case, this is a veritable chance for you to avenge.

Monster: Yes.

Oluyanju: This time, we shall know who is who.

Monster: Enough of too much talk. Let's begin.

Oluyanju: Yes, let's begin. I expect you to fire the first shot just like before.

Monster: No, you are the king now, you fire first.

Oluyanju: If that be the case, take this. *(He hurls an object like a discuss at the monster)*

Monster: Yeeeiii. What is this? *(He falls on the ground*

	and struggles to get up)
Oluyanju:	With that, you are gone forever.
Monster:	Never! I'm not a small creature to fall in easy battle like this *(He roars and gathers himself together)*
Oluyanju:	If that does not catch you...
Monster:	You won't get a chance to try the second time. (He rushes at Oluyanju, holds him by the head, lifts him up and suspends him in the air). You see yourself, a very small fry. I'll kill you now and feed your carcass to the vultures.
Oluyanju:	*(Struggles for survival.)* No not you. Not even ten thousand of you would subdue me.
Monster:	What! You still have the effrontery to talk instead of pleading for your safety.
Oluyanju:	Not from you. *(Frees himself from his grip and then hurls another object at the monster. This time hitting him in the eyes and he begins to grope)*
Monster:	My eyes! My eyes.
Oluyanju:	Serves you right.
Monster:	Look, if I get you now.
Oluyanju:	You will never get me again.
Monster:	I will crush you *(He gropes and staggers)*
Oluyanju:	Take this. *(Hits him with one heavy hammer on the head and down he goes. Quickly, Oluyanju*

removes a cutlass from his sack and severs his head from his body. He holds the head as a sign of victory, but the rest of the body begins to transform into various species of beings. This could be achieved with the aid of lights)

Chief: (Rushes in) Great king, our Great king

Guards: What is the matter?

(Oluyanju wakes up)

Chief 2: Can't you hear the sound of mutiny outside or are you deaf?

Oluyanju: Yes, what is going on?

(Mutiny sounds swell)

Chiefs: (Crowding about Oluyanju's stead) Please save our lives.

Oluyanju: Calm down and say what the matter is.

Chiefs: Great king, the whole city is under siege.

Chief 1: No, it is mutiny.

Chief 2: An uprising.

Oluyanju: Why?

Chiefs: It is the people.

Oluyanju: I thought we settled the rift for them here before they dispersed.

Guards: Yes, you did.

Oluyanju: You guards, position yourselves there, nobody

	enters this palace in a senseless haste.
Guards:	Yes, Great king. *(They positioned themselves as ordered)*
Oluyanju:	Aha, what type of lawlessness is this? *(The noise from the rioters is now disrupting proceedings in the palace).*
Chiefs:	(Now remorseful) Great king, if we do not allow them peacefully... remember, he who makes peaceful change impossible makes violent change inevitable.
Oluyanju:	They dare not try any force with me.
Chiefs:	If they do?
Oluyanju:	I will prove my mettle to them... (At that material time, the rioters rushed the guards over and entered the palace by force, advancing towards the chiefs behind Oluyanju) Stop there all of you! Where do you think you are?

(They all complied as if remote-controlled)

Oluyanju:	What is the matter with you? Why are you so unreasonable?
Masses:	We are very sorry, Great king.
Oluyanju:	Be sorry for yourselves.
Masses:	Forgive us, great one.
Oluyanju:	And if I don't?
Masses:	We are doomed, great king.

Oluyanju: How do you explain this unruly behavior of yours?

Mass I: In our excitement that we overcame all the enemies of progress in this land, we decided to come and rejoice with you.

Oluyanju: Be specific. How have you overcome?

Masses: We killed all the visible enemies, our king.

Oluyanju: You did what?!

Masses: We killed them.

Oluyanju: But why?

Masses: Our Great king, please don't be sorry for them. We learnt one thing from your action of the other time though.

Oluyanju: What did you learn from me?

Mass II: We learnt that we should be patient to listen to people talk before we carry out an action.

Oluyanju: How has that helped you?

Mass IV: When we listened to the light workers mention names of those involved in their poor service delivery, we knew it is good to always get to the bottom of a matter before taking action, otherwise only the poor souls of the electricity workers would've suffered.

Oluyanju: You killed the light workers too? Why? When? Where? Oh my God! You shouldn't have. Instead you should have incarcerated them till you get better alternatives or an improvement in their tools. If they run on water before, you make them

	try gas, or turbine or a steam or air. Better still you conduct a research of cities that are maximally effective with power, you negotiate with them at an affordable cost. Period! your action of wanton killing is barbaric and out of taste.
Mass III:	*(Remorsefully)* We are sorry. Now we understand our king.
Oluyanju:	In your blind action of massacre and genocide, who will now work your light for you? Who told you capital punishment is the way out? Why? Why did you do it?
Masses:	Only the bosses who allowed themselves to be fingered in the whole mess and did not cry out loud to be saved.
Mass I:	See Great king, these things are not new in this enclave.
Mass II:	A revolution they call it.
Mass III.	A neighbouring city to us here is now enjoying a lasting peace.
Oluyanju:	Why is that so?
Mass II:	Ours is just concentrated on the light workers and their collaborators.
Mass IV:	At least, somebody must pick up the gauntlet. Somebody must also be made a scape goat.
Masses:	You will see how the electricity will function now. Our hospitals, our banks, our small scale businesses, etc. will not have to run on generators, paying double money for a single service of light provision.

Oluyanju:	Who are the people you dealt with?
Masses:	All the people mentioned by the light worker's bosses.
Oluyanju:	I was sleeping right here on this throne before your rioting noise woke me up.
Masses:	Sorry about that Great king.
Oluyanju:	Don't bother again. Like I was saying, in my sleep, I had a dream.
Mass IV:	Sweet dreams from where our Great king?
Oluyanju:	Before I tell you what happened in my dream. Let me ask you what you intend doing with your loyal chief crouching behind me.
Mass III:	Our original intention was to discipline them like the rest of them that were found guilty, but when you restrained us, they remain covered under your tutelage.
Oluyanju:	Thank you for honouring me this much.
Mass II:	Thank you too our king.
Oluyanju:	See light in that corner over there. So, light used to come out from there too.
Mass V:	We told you light is our life.
Mass III:	This is a sign that our spiritual cleansing has paid off after all.
Masses:	See light under your throne and under your feet.

Oluyanju:	With this kind of happiness, can your chiefs join us?
Mass I:	If you so wish, our king.
Oluyanju:	What about you people? Don't you wish so?
Masses:	Your wish is our command.
Oluyanju:	Thank you once again
Chiefs:	Thank you beautiful people. Thank you our king.
Oluyanju:	Thank you for thanking me.
Mass VI:	We are still in suspense- about your dream.
Oluyanju:	There is no suspense about it than I fought a terrible beast and I conquered it.
Mass I:	Hey!!! The same victory we achieved in real life. See.
Oluyanju:	Besides, the striking feature of my conquest and your victory is that, when I killed the monster and beheaded it, the rest of its body began to change to the people you said you killed in real life.
Mass V:	So, why are we not going to rejoice, the good people with their good king have conquered. So, bye-bye to strife, bye-bye to corruption.

(Everybody in the palace joins in the celebration song. The masses go to fetch the king from the throne area. They dance round him and hand in hand like a victory song, sang to "stand up" "Standup for the Champion". This persists, Oluyanju orders the guards to supply drinks to everybody. In a jiffy, it is carried out).

Oluyanju: Serve everybody round.

Guards: It shall be done, your highness.

Chiefs: That's the spirit, Great king.

Masses: Our Great king, you are the one for us.

Chiefs: You sure understand this people well.

Oluyanju: If a people know what is right and they do just that for the collective good of all, then there is no other reward for goodness other than goodness. Let them merry!

Masses: Koro kokokoko kenkuku eeeeiii!!!

Oluyanju: What is the meaning? What are they saying?

Chiefs: They are saying they haven't seen a more powerful or a livelier and a more important king like this before.

Mass IV: Great king, we will drink to stupor here because it is from you.

Oluyanju: That is my style Rejoice and be merry.

(The singing and the dancing resume. This time around, a wild and an ecstatic dance, but they excuse the king to sit down on his throne and watch and appreciate their culture. The king becomes too excited and carried away that he asks that more palm wine should be served him. In his ecstasy, he laughs heartily as he appreciates the dancers until the wine chokes him and he coughs aloud attracting the attention of merry makers.)

Masses: Are you alright, Great king?

Chiefs:	*(Attending to him)* Be quite now, Great king. Do not try to say anything or force yourself to breath.
Mass II:	Hit him lightly on the back of the head.
Mass III:	Nobody dares do that.
Mass II:	Then pat him on the back in a rocking manner.
Chief I:	He is a king.
Mass II:	So, that is why he should die carelessly?
Mass III:	Let somebody give him a helping hand, he must not die.
Mass Iv:	Not even today, the greatest day in our history.
Chief I:	*(Pats him on the back.)* What's his name?
Chief II:	Why his name? What for?
Chief I:	So that I call it and he is revived.
Chief II:	Just say Great king. He'll answer you.
Chief I:	G-R-E-A-T king, G-R-E-A-T king.
Masses:	What is this? He is choking the more.
Chiefs:	Let everybody go home. Whoever has a sure medicine for his cure should run home to bring it.

(Everybody except the guards and chiefs vamooses)

Chief I:	What do we do?
Chief II:	We stay to revive him of course
Chief I:	He does not stand a chance of survival.
Chief II:	That means we are both doomed.

Chief I:	The masses will strangle us.
Guards:	Our Great king will live.
Chiefs:	Shut up! Now go inside and look for what to use on him quick.
Guards:	Okay chiefs.
Chief II:	I feel like running away.
Chief I:	To where?
Chief II:	To where my legs can take me. At least, it won't be said of me that I'm daft to the point of running into my death trap.
Chief I:	Mark you, this king is very powerful
Chief II:	Yes I know.
Chief I:	What if he is only pretending and recording our actions?
Chief II:	That is a case of the devil and the deep blue sea.
Chief I:	A choice must be made between an imminent death and precarious one.
Chief II:	Between a cruel death and a mild one.
Chief I:	Between a big death and a small one.
Chief II:	Between a fast death and a slow one.
Chief I:	Honestly, this king's sudden illness precipitates further crisis instead of solving the one on ground.
Chief II:	In that case, let us embark on our escape journey early.
Chief I:	What are we waiting for?

(They hold hands and tiptoed outside. Light fades.)

Light gradually begins to illuminate the stage. This time around, we go back to the first scene where the doctor and others are trying to revive Oluyanju

Adunni: Hey! Doctor, see he is moving.

Doctor: I told you

Neighbour I: We thank goodness.

Neighbour II: That we are not struck with calamity in this compound on account of Mr. Oluyanju is enough to give thanks and praises.

Doctor: But it's not yet uhuru.

Everybody: What again doctor?

Doctor: He is still in coma.

Neighbour I: But he will be revived eventually.

Doctor: He is alive already

Adunni: (Burst into tears) praise God!

Neighbours: Halleluyah!

Adunni: Praise God! (Wiping her tears)

Doctor: Allahu Akbar

Neighbours: Amin

Doctor: We need to give him insulin oxygen to prod his brains properly

Adunni: Where can I get that to buy?

Neighbour I: But it is midnight already.

Neighbour II: You cannot get any of the shops to open for you at

49

	this eleventh hour.
Doctor:	I have not even said anybody should go and buy anything.
Adunni:	It was because you said he would need oxygen.
Doctor:	But you didn't bother to ask me perhaps I have it or not.
Neighbour I:	We are sorry.
Neighbour II:	We are only eager to see him well. That's why.
Doctor:	Never mind. I have all that in my first Aid Box here. So, I will.....(Momentarily, light just comes on)
Everybody:	Up NEPA!
Oluyanju:	(Gets up suddenly.) Henh! What is that?
Everybody:	Praaaaaaaise God! *(The reverberating sound nearly brings the house down so much so that the children and other neighbours join them in fear)*
Oluyanju:	Have they finished dancing?
Adunni:	Who are the ones dancing?
Doctor:	Leave him alone for now.
Neighbour III:	He must have sojourned wide. What really happened to him?
Neighbour II:	He had been unconscious since yester-night
Children:	What?! Our daddy.

Adunni: Yes, your daddy.

Children: But we chatted with him yesterday before we went to bed.

Oluyanju: My chiefs, where are the guards?

Doctor: Just leave him he will be okay.

Adunni: Hope he won't run mental?

Doctor: Never! I will give him some drugs. In about a few hours, he will be okay.

(Light goes off again)

Everybody: Ah! NEPA!

Neighbour II: But how long will this nonsense by NEPA last?

Neighbour I: Tell me something. Have you ever taken a stroll at late nights or midnight or even at dawn when there is no power? A sorry tale, a complete stone age story.

Neighbour II: Yet some of our influencial country men and women pride themselves as being rich instead of burying their heads in the sand and covering their faces in shame.

Neighbour III: Right from my childhood, my father had hoped NEPA will improve, now I'm a grown up I'm hoping NEPA will improve. What day really, what year will it be, is it till thy kingdom come?

Neighbour I: Sometimes, I wonder if generation yet unborn will not consider it a fairy tale, this issue of NEPA: paying for energy not consumed, paying for services not rendered, yet nobody dares challenge and win government in this part of the world. In the midst of educated citizens, these anomalies persist. Just like some stories in the holy books. They just fondle with the switch ON

& OFF as if it were a toy. Those of them who did not have access to toys in their infancy.

Neighbour III: At a time when the country clamours for foreign investments, which foreign investor would risk his resources in this 'lightless' country. Yet we can be more advantageous than China if light stays.

Neighbour II: Perhaps we should even change their name to- NEVER EXPECT POWER ALWAYS. Instead of- NATIONAL ELECTRIC POWER AUTHORITY. *(At that instance, NEPA Just restores light. We hear UP NEPA from off stage. The actors stare at each other's faces, speechless and the stage light fades finally).*

Curtain drops.

Play Ends.

To God be the Glory.

Back drop of Sango's (god of thunder's) large frame i.e. king-size of it should be displayed mostly in the scenes and most likely in the home of the Oluyanjus.

I have endeavoured not to localize the play in any given tribe in Nigeria even though, it is a Nigerian story. But the strong bond of my tribe and my ethnic conviction have both overwhelmed me into settling for only two Yoruba names in the character personae: Oluyanju and his wife Adunni. However, the two traditional (native) names can be substituted for any suitable names of convenience for the Director of the piece.

www.ingramcontent.com/pod-product-compliance
Lightning Source LLC
Chambersburg PA
CBHW051704040426
42446CB00009B/1290